EXCLUSIVE

ELEVATE

TAKE YOUR BUSINESS
TO NEW HEIGHTS

VIKKIMJONES.COM

*Practice daily mindfulness exercises.
*Engage in regular physical activity that you enjoy.
*Prioritize activities that make you feel rejuvenated.
*Set boundaries and say no to commitments that drain your energy or do not align with your priorities.
PRIORITIZE
SELF CARE
GUIDE & WORKBOOK
WRITTEN BY
VIKKI JONES
Walmart
BARNES&NOBLE
BOOKSELLERS
amazon.com
BAM!
BOOKS·A·MILLION

Editor's Note

Dear Readers,

As we embark on the 44th issue of VMH Magazine, I am thrilled to bring you a special feature that celebrates the incredible achievements of entrepreneurs like you. This issue is dedicated to acknowledging the hard work, dedication, and sacrifices that you have made on your journey towards success.

In this issue, we dive deep into the theme of "It's Your Time: Embrace the Rewards You've Earned." It is a reminder that after all the hustle and bustle, the time has come for you to revel in the fruits of your labor. This feature serves as a celebration of your accomplishments and a testament to the power of perseverance.

We understand the challenges you have faced, the tears shed, and the emotional rollercoaster you have endured. Yet, through it all, you have always pushed forward, allowing growth to take its course. You have discounted your rates, selflessly supporting others in their pursuit of success. You have poured your heart and soul into your businesses, and now it is time for you to enjoy all the rewards that await.

As we commence a new year, it is the perfect time to reflect on how far you have come. The 44th issue of VMH Magazine is here to remind you of your worth, your value, and the unique contributions you bring to the world. It is a call to embrace the opportunities that come your way and to believe in yourself and your abilities.

But amidst the celebration of your achievements, I want to pose a question: Are you ready to write your book? Writing a book can open a world of opportunity for you as an entrepreneur. It allows you to share your expertise, your experiences, and your unique insights with a wider audience. It is a chance to leave a lasting legacy and establish yourself as a thought leader in your industry.

So, as you immerse yourself in the pages of this issue, I encourage you to take a moment to celebrate your own journey. Acknowledge the sacrifices you have made, the growth you have experienced, and the successes you have achieved. Embrace the fact that it is your time to enjoy all the rewards that await you.

As we begin this new year together, let us embrace the spirit of gratitude and excitement. Let us believe in ourselves, trust in the journey we have taken, and savor the abundance that is ready to flow into our lives. May this issue of VMH Magazine serve as a beacon of inspiration, reminding us all that our hard work and dedication have not gone unnoticed.

Thank you for being a part of our VMH Magazine community. We are honored to share this journey with you, and we look forward to witnessing your continued growth

Vikki Jones

Editor-in-Chief

CONTENTS

VMH Magazine Created & Designed by Vikki Jones
Cover Image: Vikki Jones
Photography Credit: Garry Jones

THE HOUSE WITH A BIG HEART

Montréal, Canada

Entre Quatre Murs unveils its design of The House with a Big Heart, located in Town of Mount Royal, in Montreal. Originally built in 1959, the house had not been renovated for several decades and featured typical enclosed rooms and small, narrow, dark hallways. The clients wanted to create a home that would fit their lifestyle. They chose to purchase the property for its location and large garden, but wanted a radical transformation of all its floors so that their young family could thrive within its walls for many years to come.

Photo Credits: Phil Bernard

Photo Credit: Phil Bernard
via VRCOM

ENTRE QUATRE MURS, UNVEILED THEIR ARCHITECTURAL MASTERPIECE
THE HOUSE WITH THE BIG HEART

WRITTEN BY VIKKI JONES

Montreal's Town of Mount Royal has recently become home to a remarkable architectural gem that is captivating the attention of design enthusiasts. Entre Quatre Murs, a renowned design studio, has unveiled their masterpiece: The House with the Big Heart. Originally constructed in 1959, this house had long been in need of renovation. With its enclosed rooms and narrow, dark hallways, it lacked the openness and functionality desired by its new owners.

The clients, a young family, saw the potential in this property due to its prime location and spacious garden. They sought a radical transformation that would allow them to thrive within these walls for years to come. And Entre Quatre Murs delivered.

To address the lack of natural light, the design team adopted an ingenious approach. They decompartmentalized many of the rooms and created a stunning opening between the first and second floors. As soon as one enters the house, they are greeted by a completely open, white wooden staircase with glass railings that span all three floors. This architectural marvel not only adds an element of lightness but also allows sunlight to permeate throughout the entire house. Additionally, wide openings were made on the rear facade, offering breathtaking views of the garden from every floor.

While the house boasts an open concept layout, careful consideration was given to ensure each room maintains its privacy. Gatline Artis, the owner of the house and designer at Entre Quatre Murs, explains, "We wanted each room to have its privacy, and the views between each space not to detract from the enjoyment of the moment, but simply to allow glimpses of other family members moving from room to room." This design choice provides a sense of calm and privacy within the larger open plan.

The kitchen design takes an unconventional yet captivating approach. Divided into two separate spaces, the front portion consists of three integrated furniture elements that exude lightness and refinement, reminiscent of the living room's bookcases. The absence of wall cabinets emphasizes openness, while delicate legs on the island create a communal table area for family gatherings. Behind the front portion lies an all-black pantry, which creates a striking contrast and discreetly integrates the refrigerator, coffee corner, and small daily appliances. This harmonious combination of aesthetics and functionality perfectly embodies the essence of family life.

On the second floor, private spaces revolve around the central opening of the house. Rather than traditional corridors and partitioned areas, this innovative configuration immerses occupants in the heart of family life as soon as they leave their private spaces. The inclusion of an office as a central piece in the floor plan demonstrates the owners' commitment to their daily work routines. Placed at the center of the space, the large work surfaces act as a central island where the entire family can gather, including the children during homework time.

Even the basement showcases meticulous design choices. Three distinct functions coexist harmoniously without overlapping, thanks to the use of cabinetry modules that visually delineate the gym, pool area, and family room. Custom-made furniture maximizes space utilization while enhancing the functionality of each sub-space. It has truly transformed the basement into a vibrant and multifunctional area enjoyed by the entire family.

Gatline Artis reflects on the journey of creating their dream home: "We were looking for a sweet home, a little cocoon where we could see our children grow up, but above all, we wanted a home that reflected our own image. Creating our own completely bespoke home, in which we could live and thrive for decades to come, was paramount." The process was undoubtedly laborious but immensely rewarding. Each passing season continues to amaze them, exceeding their expectations of functionality and quality of life.

The House with the Big Heart, also known as Dobie, has been recognized with six Gold Certifications at the Grands Prix du Design - 16th edition. It stands as a testament to Entre Quatre Murs' commitment to crafting unique and timeless living spaces. Functionality, materiality, and light serve as the studio's guiding principles, ensuring that their designs enhance the comfort and well-being of their clients.

Beyond design and interior architecture, Entre Quatre Murs believes in creating spaces that evoke deep emotions and truly reflect their clients' identities. Their tight-knit team of talented designers consistently delivers excellence, redefining the concept of "home" on a daily basis.

While the house boasts an open concept layout, careful consideration was given to ensure each room maintains its privacy. Gatline Artis, the owner of the house and designer at Entre Quatre Murs, explains, "We wanted each room to have its privacy, and the views between each space not to detract from the enjoyment of the moment, but simply to allow glimpses of other family members moving from room to room." This design choice provides a sense of calm and privacy within the larger open plan.

Discover Your Inner Author and Tell Your Story!

Your story, your voice, expertly crafted.

1. Personalized Writing Coaching: Our writing coaches will work closely with you, asking a curated list of questions to understand the story you want to tell. With your answers as a guide, we'll help you develop your book, ensuring your personality, voice, and tone shine through.

2. Professional Ghostwriting: Don't have the time or confidence to write your book? Our skilled ghostwriters will transform your ideas and experiences into a captivating manuscript. We'll capture your essence, crafting a book that feels authentically yours.

3. Expert Guidance: Whether you choose writing coaching or ghostwriting, our team will provide expert guidance throughout the process. From outlining and structuring your book to refining the final draft, we'll be there to support you and ensure your vision is realized.

Ready to see your story in print? Visit www.VMHPublishing.net or call 917-409-7420 to learn more about our writing coach and ghostwriting services. Start your journey towards becoming a published author today!

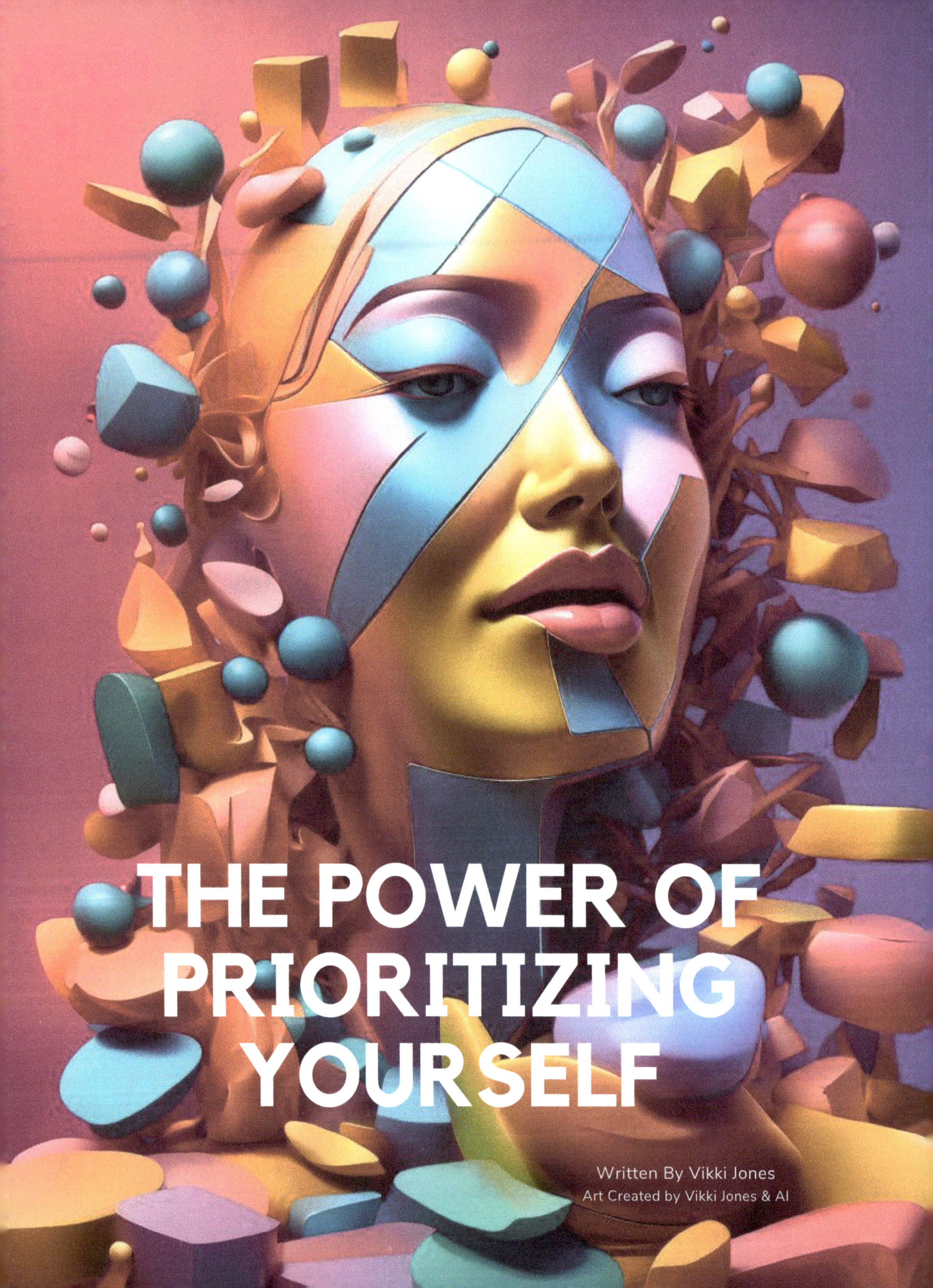

THE POWER OF PRIORITIZING YOURSELF
Written By Vikki Jones
Art Created by Vikki Jones & AI

THE BENEFITS OF BEING INTENTIONAL ABOUT PRIORITIZING YOURSELF

In a fast-paced world filled with endless responsibilities and commitments, it's easy to get caught up in the chaos and neglect our own well-being. However, it is essential to make a conscious effort to put ourselves first and be intentional about it. Prioritizing self-care and personal growth not only benefits us individually but also positively impacts our relationships, productivity, and overall happiness. In this article, we will explore the numerous advantages of making it a point to put ourselves first and how it can transform our lives for the better.

1. Improved Mental and Emotional Well-being:

By intentionally prioritizing ourselves, we create space for self-reflection and self-awareness. Taking time to nurture our mental and emotional health allows us to recharge, reduce stress, and gain clarity. Engaging in activities such as meditation, journaling, or pursuing hobbies that bring us joy can significantly improve our overall well-being.

2. Enhanced Physical Health:

Neglecting our physical health can have detrimental effects on our overall quality of life. Making ourselves a priority means carving out time for regular exercise, eating well-balanced meals, and getting enough sleep. Prioritizing physical well-being not only boosts our energy levels but also strengthens our immune system and reduces the risk of chronic diseases.

3. Increased Productivity:

Contrary to popular belief, putting ourselves first does not equate to being selfish. By taking care of our physical and mental needs, we are better equipped to handle the demands of daily life. When we prioritize self-care, we enhance our focus, creativity, and problem-solving abilities, leading to increased productivity and efficiency in both personal and professional spheres.

4. Enhanced Relationships:

When we neglect ourselves, our relationships may suffer. By intentionally putting ourselves first, we set a positive example for those around us. Prioritizing self-care teaches others the importance of valuing their own well-being and encourages healthier boundaries. By nurturing ourselves, we become more present, compassionate, and better able to connect with others on a deeper level.

5. Increased Happiness and Fulfillment:

Putting ourselves first and being intentional about it ultimately leads to greater happiness and fulfillment. When we prioritize our needs, we engage in activities that bring us joy and align with our values. This, in turn, leads to a greater sense of purpose and contentment in our lives.

Making it a point to put ourselves first and being intentional about self-care is crucial for our overall well-being. By prioritizing ourselves, we improve our mental, emotional, and physical health. Additionally, we enhance our productivity, strengthen our relationships, and ultimately experience greater happiness and fulfillment.

Remember, self-care is not selfish; it is a necessary investment in our own growth and happiness. So, let us make a conscious decision to prioritize ourselves and reap the abundant benefits that come with it.

KORI COLEMAN: EMPOWERING OTHERS TO ACHIEVE SUCCESS AND AUTHENTICITY

WRITTEN BY VIKKI JONES
PHOTO COURTESY OF KORI COLEMAN

At just 22 years old, Kori Coleman is already making waves in the literary world with his book "BOSS UP." But his achievements extend far beyond his writing. As a student, part-time employee, and aspiring entrepreneur, Coleman embodies the values of dedication and determination. Growing up in a military family and experiencing life in various parts of the South and Washington state, Coleman's diverse background has shaped his perspective and inspired him to share his wisdom with others.

The Power of "BOSS UP":

In his book "BOSS UP," Coleman combines personal anecdotes and valuable life lessons to guide readers on their journeys to success. He emphasizes the importance of making calculated moves and taking proactive steps towards achieving personal and professional goals. Drawing from his experience as a boxer, Coleman encourages readers to stay prepared and ready for the opportunities that come their way.

Moving in Silence: Protecting Your Energy:

One of the recurring themes in Coleman's book is the concept of moving in silence. He firmly believes that not everyone should be privy to one's plans. Coleman recognizes that envy can lead to attempts to sabotage what you've built, and revealing your plans may invite imitation. He values protecting his energy from negative influences and considers keeping his endeavors private as crucial to his recipe for success.

Coleman explains, "Not everyone should be privy to your plans, as envy can lead to attempts to sabotage what you've built. Additionally, revealing plans may invite imitation, and I value protecting my energy from negative influences. Keeping my endeavors private is crucial to my recipe for success."

The Power of Authenticity:

In his book, Coleman also emphasizes the importance of staying authentic despite the challenges that come with it. He acknowledges that criticism and adversity are inevitable but highlights the role of resilience in navigating these obstacles. Coleman finds strength in the support of those closest to him, which helps him stay grounded and true to himself amidst challenges.

Coleman shares his thoughts on authenticity, saying, "Staying authentic has its challenges, but I've navigated criticism and adversity by embracing resilience. The support of those closest to me keeps me grounded. Despite facing unwanted criticism, my dedication to sharing my message and mastering resilience helps me stay true to myself amidst challenges."

Inspiring Others to Boss Up:

As Kori Coleman continues to make his mark in the literary world, it is evident that his passion for empowering others shines through in every aspect of his life. "BOSS UP" serves as a valuable resource for readers to navigate their own paths towards success. Coleman's story is an inspiration to those who dare to dream big and are willing to put in the work to achieve their goals. Coleman's book, combined with his personal experiences and insights, motivates readers to embrace their unique journeys and create the future they desire. As he shares his journey and lessons learned, Coleman empowers others to take charge of their lives and make a lasting impact on the world.

Through "BOSS UP," Coleman provides readers with the tools and motivation to navigate their own paths towards success. By emphasizing the importance of moving in silence, protecting one's energy, and staying authentic, Coleman inspires readers to overcome challenges and stay true to themselves.

As Kori Coleman continues to inspire and empower others, his dedication to making a difference is evident. With his book and unwavering commitment, Coleman reminds us that age is not a barrier to success. With determination, hard work, and a commitment to authenticity, anyone can achieve greatness. Kori Coleman is a rising star, inspiring others to boss up and create the future they want.

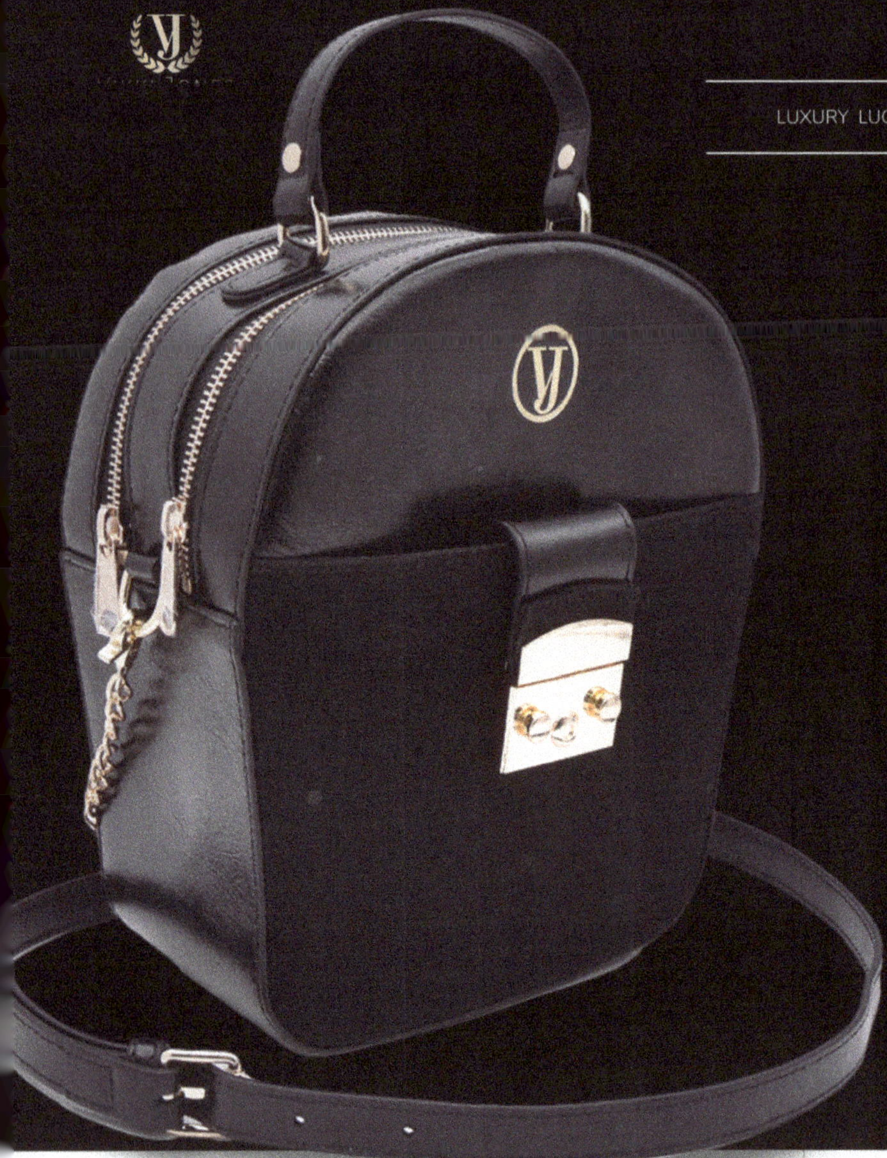

VIKKI JONES

DESIGNER

COMFORTABLE
CARRYING OPTIONS

Say goodbye to uncomfortable bags. Vikki Jones' designs prioritize comfort, with padded straps, ergonomic handles, and lightweight construction, ensuring a comfortable carrying experience even during long journeys.

Need extra space? Jones' bags feature expandable compartments, allowing you to increase the capacity when needed. Travel with confidence, knowing you have room for souvenirs or extra work documents.

VIKKIJONES.COM

Embrace Your Potential and Achieve Extraordinary Success

Written by Vikki Jones

In a world filled with immense possibilities and endless opportunities, it is disheartening to witness countless individuals holding themselves back from realizing their full potential. Far too often, self-doubt and fear of failure prevent us from taking that leap of faith and embracing our greatness. But what if, just for a moment, we set aside our doubts and allowed ourselves to truly explore our strengths, talents, and unique abilities? What if we dared to think outside of the box and invested in our belief in ourselves? The results could be nothing short of extraordinary.

Each one of us possesses an incredible reservoir of untapped potential. However, it is only by giving ourselves a chance that we can unlock this hidden greatness. It begins with a journey inward, a sincere examination of our strengths and talents. By identifying and developing these strong points, we lay the foundation for our success.

Think of yourself as a diamond in the rough. You have the potential to shine brilliantly, but it requires effort, patience, and a willingness to invest in self-improvement. Take the time to discover what truly brings you joy and fulfillment. Nurture those passions and talents, for they are the keys to unlocking your greatness.

It is also crucial to break free from the confines of conventional thinking. The world is changing rapidly, and the most successful individuals are those who can adapt and think outside of the box.

Embrace innovation, challenge the status quo, and be unafraid to take calculated risks. By doing so, you open up a world of possibilities and pave the way for greatness to flow into your life.

However, none of this is possible without a strong belief in oneself. Confidence is the driving force behind every successful person. Believe in your abilities, your dreams, and your potential. Surround yourself with positive influences, seek out mentors who can guide you, and never underestimate the power of self-affirmation.

It is important to recognize that greatness does not come easily or overnight. It is a journey, filled with obstacles and setbacks. But it is through these challenges that we grow, learn, and become stronger. Embrace failure as a stepping stone to success and never let setbacks deter you from pursuing your dreams.

So, I implore you to give yourself a chance. Look deep within, develop your strong points, and allow yourself the opportunity to think outside of the box. Invest in and strengthen your belief in yourself. Know that you have what it takes to be great. Believe it, embrace it, and watch as your greatness flows effortlessly into every aspect of your life.

Embrace the rewards that are coming your way and savor every moment.

"..let's be clear - this is not about selfishness or abandoning the principles that have guided you... It's a celebration of all that you've accomplished and an invitation to step into a new chapter of your life.."

- Vikki Jones

Receive your abundance.

– @iamvikkijones

It's your time. After all the hard work, dedication, and sacrifices you've made, it's finally time for you to step into the spotlight and receive the rewards you deserve. You've put in the effort, going above and beyond expectations, and now it's time to see the fruits of your labor.

You've poured your heart and soul into your company, always pushing forward and allowing growth to take its course. You've discounted your rates, selflessly helping others fulfill their dreams. You've shed tears, endured the rollercoaster of entrepreneurship, and yet you persevered, staying focused on your goals.

You've put in the work, and now it's time to reap the benefits. No longer do you need to wait in the shadows; it's time for you to step into the spotlight and shine. The stage is set for you to receive the recognition and success you've worked so hard for.

You've honed your skills, developed your talents, and made countless sacrifices along the way. Your dedication and commitment have paved the way for this moment. It's time to embrace the rewards that are rightfully yours.

But let's be clear - this is not about selfishness or abandoning the principles that have guided you. It's about acknowledging your worth, recognizing your value, and allowing yourself to receive the abundance that is meant for you. It's a celebration of all that you've accomplished and an invitation to step into a new chapter of your life.

As you embark on this exciting phase, remember that it's not just about material rewards. It's also about finding fulfillment, joy, and a sense of purpose. It's about aligning your passions and interests with your work, so that every day feels like a gift.

Your journey has led you to this moment, and now it's time to embrace the opportunities that come your way. Trust in yourself and your abilities. Believe that you are deserving of the success and happiness that awaits you.

This editorial is not meant to advise you on what to do; it is simply stating the fact that it's your time. It's a reminder to acknowledge your achievements, celebrate your growth, and step into the greatness that is waiting for you. your greatness.

So, my fellow entrepreneur, take a moment to reflect on how far you've come. Recognize the hard work, determination, and resilience that have brought you to this point. And then, with a sense of gratitude and excitement, open yourself up to the abundance that is ready to flow into your life.

It's your time to receive, to thrive, and to shine. Embrace the rewards that are coming your way and savor every moment. Your hard work has paid off, and now it's time to enjoy the fruits of your labor. Believe in yourself, trust in the journey you've taken, and know that you are deserving of all the success and happiness that is coming your way. It's your time, and the world is ready to witness your greatness.

LUXURY
CREATIONS
VIKKIJONES.COM

ARE READY TO WRITE YOUR BOOK

———

The world of literature is a vast and captivating realm that allows authors to share their unique perspectives, stories, and knowledge with readers across the globe. If you've ever felt the burning desire to write a book, now is the perfect time to embark on your authorial journey. In this article, we'll explore the excitement, challenges, and rewards that come with writing a book. So, are you ready to dive into the realm of words and create a masterpiece of your own?

Unleashing Your Creativity:
Writing a book is a powerful outlet for your creativity. It allows you to express your thoughts, emotions, and experiences in a way that resonates with readers. Whether you have a fictional tale brewing in your mind or a non-fiction book idea that can enlighten others, the act of writing enables you to let your imagination soar and bring your ideas to life.

Finding Your Writing Process:
Discovering your unique writing process is a crucial step in the journey of writing a book. Some authors thrive in organized environments, meticulously outlining their chapters and characters before diving into the writing process. Others prefer a more spontaneous approach, allowing the story to unfold naturally as they write. Experiment with different methods and find the writing process that best suits your style and fuels your creativity.

Overcoming Challenges:
Writing a book is not without its challenges. It requires discipline, dedication, and perseverance. Writer's block, self-doubt, and time management can all pose obstacles along the way. However, by adopting strategies such as setting writing goals, creating a writing routine, and seeking support from fellow writers or writing communities, you can overcome these challenges and keep your creative momentum flowing.

Writing is a powerful tool for communication, bridging gaps and connecting people across time and space. Whether you're sharing stories, ideas, or knowledge, writing allows you to convey your message with clarity and precision. Through your words, you can touch the hearts and minds of readers.

Crafting Memorable Characters and Engaging Plots:
One of the most thrilling aspects of writing a book is the opportunity to create memorable characters and captivating plots. Dive deep into character development, breathing life into your protagonists and antagonists. Craft a compelling plot that keeps readers turning pages, eager to unravel the twists and turns of your story. With each word, you have the power to transport readers to new worlds and evoke emotions that linger long after the final page.

Navigating the Publishing Landscape:
Once your manuscript is complete, the next step is to navigate the publishing landscape. Traditional publishing, self-publishing, and hybrid publishing are all viable options, each with its own advantages and considerations. Research the different paths, weigh the pros and cons, and choose the publishing route that aligns with your goals and aspirations as an author.

Sharing Your Book with the World:
Publishing your book is just the beginning. The joy of writing is in sharing your creation with the world. Engage in book launches, author readings, and literary events to connect with readers and build your author brand. Leverage the power of social media and online platforms to expand your reach and engage with a global audience. Embrace the feedback and reviews, as they provide valuable insights and fuel your growth as an author.

Embarking on the journey of writing a book is an exhilarating endeavor that opens doors to endless possibilities. It allows you to leave a lasting impact on readers, share your unique voice, and contribute to the rich tapestry of literature. So, are you ready to embrace your authorial journey? Grab your pen, unleash your creativity, and let the words flow onto the pages. Your book awaits and the world is ready to be captivated by your story.

(Family Features) Between work, family obligations and a constantly changing world, people in the United States are stressed. In fact, U.S. workers are among the most stressed in the world, according to a State of the Global Workplace study. While some stress is unavoidable and can be good for you, constant or chronic stress can have real consequences for your mental and physical health.

Chronic stress can increase your lifetime risk of heart disease and stroke. It can also lead to unhealthy habits like overeating, physical inactivity and smoking while also increasing risk factors, including high blood pressure, depression and anxiety. However, a scientific statement from the American Heart Association shows reducing stress and cultivating a positive mindset can improve health and well-being.

To help people understand the connection between stress and physical health, the American Heart Association offers these science-backed insights to help reduce chronic stress.

Stay Active
Exercise is one of the easiest ways to keep your body healthy and release stress. Physical activity is linked to lower risk of diseases, stronger bones and muscles, improved mental health and cognitive function and lower risk of depression. It can also help increase energy and improve quality of sleep. The American Heart Association recommends adults get at least 150 minutes per week of moderate-intensity activity, 75 minutes of vigorous activity or a combination.

Meditate
Incorporate meditation and mindfulness practices into your day to give yourself a few minutes to create some distance from daily stress. Some studies show meditation can reduce blood pressure, improve sleep, support the immune system and increase your ability to process information.

Practice Positivity
A positive mindset can improve overall health. Studies show a positive mindset can help you live longer, and happy individuals tend to sleep better, exercise more, eat better and not smoke. Practice

5 HEALTHY HABITS TO HELP REDUCE STRESS

positive self-talk to help you stay calm. Instead of saying, "everything is going wrong," re-frame the situation and remind yourself "I can handle this if I take it one step at a time."

Show Gratitude
Gratitude – or thankfulness – is a powerful tool that can reduce levels of depression and anxiety and improve sleep. Start by simply writing down three things you're grateful for each day.

Find a Furry Friend
Having a pet may help you get more fit; lower stress, blood pressure, cholesterol and blood sugar; and boost overall happiness and well-being. When you see, touch, hear or talk to companion animals, you may feel a sense of goodwill, joy, nurturing and happiness. At the same time, stress hormones are suppressed. Dog ownership is also associated with a lower risk of depression, according to research published by the American Heart Association.

Find more stress-management tips at Heart.org/stress.

Stress 101

Understanding stress is an important step in managing and reducing it. Consider these things to know about stress and how it could affect your life:
- Today, 1 in 3 adults in the U.S. report being worried or depressed.
- Higher levels of the stress hormone cortisol are linked to increased risk of high blood pressure and cardiovascular events like heart disease and stroke.
- The top sources of stress are money, work, family responsibilities and health concerns.
- Work-related stress is associated with a 40% increased risk of cardiovascular disease like heart attack and stroke.

The Power of SMEs: Adapting to Global Solutions

By Vikki Jones

Small and Medium-sized Enterprises (SMEs) play a vital role in the global economy, driving innovation, job creation, and economic growth. However, in times of disruption and uncertainty, such as the recent COVID-19 pandemic, these enterprises often face immense challenges that can threaten their survival. It is crucial to recognize the importance of supporting and strengthening SMEs, particularly when it comes to building resilient supply chains.

Building a resilient supply chain within SMEs is a critical aspect that deserves attention. SMEs often find themselves vulnerable to disruptions caused by various factors, including economic downturns, natural disasters, trade restrictions, and logistical challenges. These disruptions can have far-reaching consequences, impacting not only the SMEs themselves but also the larger economy.

Therefore, it is paramount to enhance the resilience of SMEs and their supply chains. This can be achieved through proactive measures and strategic planning. Governments, policymakers, and industry leaders must come together to develop supportive policies, establish risk management frameworks, and foster collaborations between SMEs and larger enterprises. By doing so, we can create an environment that enables SMEs to thrive, even in the face of adversity.

One crucial aspect of building resilient supply chains for SMEs is diversification. Relying on a single supplier or market can expose SMEs to substantial risks if disruption occurs. Encouraging SMEs to diversify their suppliers and customer bases can help mitigate these risks and ensure a more robust supply chain. By expanding their networks and exploring new markets, SMEs can decrease their dependence on a single source of revenue, enhancing their ability to adapt to changing circumstances.

Moreover, leveraging technology and digital solutions can significantly enhance both the efficiency and resilience of SMEs. Embracing e-commerce platforms, cloud-based systems, and digital communication tools can enable SMEs to streamline operations, access new markets, and expand their reach.

Technology can also facilitate real-time data tracking, allowing SMEs to identify vulnerabilities in their supply chains and take proactive measures to address them swiftly. Implementing innovative technologies provides SMEs with the agility necessary to navigate disruptions and maintain their competitiveness in the global market.

Another crucial aspect to consider is access to finance. SMEs often face constraints when seeking funding to invest in technology, expand their operations, or withstand economic shocks. Governments and financial institutions need to provide tailored financial services and support mechanisms specifically designed for SMEs. Implementing programs that offer flexible financing options, grants, and business development services can empower SMEs to invest in their growth and resilience.

Prioritizing the resilience of SMEs and building robust supply chains is of utmost importance for economic stability and growth. By adopting proactive measures such as diversification, leveraging technology, and ensuring access to finance, we can safeguard the sustainability of SMEs and strengthen their contributions to the economy. Collaboration between governments, policymakers, industry leaders, and SMEs themselves will be pivotal in creating an environment that fosters resilience and empowers the backbone of our economy. With the right support, SMEs can effectively adapt to global solutions, driving forward progress and overcoming challenges presented by an ever-changing world.creating an environment that fosters resilience and empowers them further.

Key Tips for Enhancing SMEs and Building Strong Supply Chains

1. Diversify Suppliers and Customer Bases: Encourage SMEs to expand their networks and explore new markets to reduce reliance on a single supplier or customer. By diversifying, SMEs can mitigate risks and build a more robust supply chain that can adapt to changing circumstances.

2. Embrace Technology and Digital Solutions: SMEs should leverage e-commerce platforms, cloud-based systems, and digital communication tools to streamline operations, access new markets, and enhance efficiency. Implementing innovative technologies enables SMEs to stay agile and competitive in the global market.

3. Focus on Risk Management and Planning: Governments, policymakers, and industry leaders must collaborate to develop supportive policies and risk management frameworks. Proactive planning ensures SMEs have the necessary tools to anticipate and navigate disruptions effectively.

4. Ensure Access to Finance: Tailored financial services and support mechanisms should be provided by governments and financial institutions. Flexible financing options, grants, and business development services empower SMEs to invest in their growth and resilience, strengthening their contributions to the economy.

5. Foster Collaborative Relationships: Encourage collaboration between SMEs and larger enterprises to share resources, knowledge, and expertise. Such partnerships can lead to innovative solutions, foster resilience, and create an environment where SMEs can thrive even in challenging times.

By following these key tips, SMEs can enhance their ability to adapt, build resilient supply chains, and continue driving innovation, job creation, and economic growth in the global economy.

the resilience of the human spirit

"Overcoming Trauma" is a testament to the power of personal storytelling and the transformative nature of resilience.

OVERCOMING TRAUMA

WRITTEN BY
VIKKI HANKINS

Product Details:
ISBN-13: 9798985334968
Publisher: VMH Publishing
Publication date: 11/16/2023
Pages: 552
Product Weight: 1.4 lbs.
Product Dimensions: 5.50(w) x 8.50(h) x 1.23(d)

"Overcoming Trauma" is a testament to the resilience of the human spirit. Vikki Hankins' honest and introspective memoir serves as a beacon of hope for those who have experienced their own traumas, showing that it is possible to rise above the darkest moments and reclaim one's life. Her powerful story reminds us that through self-reflection, acceptance, and the courage to confront our pain, we can find the strength to heal and truly live again. "Overcoming Trauma" is a testament to the power of personal storytelling and the transformative nature of resilience.

EMBRACING COURAGE TO CONQUER TRAUMA

In a world where trauma often leaves deep scars, recognizing the transformative potential of courage involves facing our pain and releasing what no longer serves us. However, it is important to be mindful that healing is a process and not a 'one-size-fits-all' solution.

In the depths of trauma, it is the unwavering courage of the human spirit that propels individuals forward, enabling them to conquer the most formidable challenges. Vikki Hankins' memoir, "Overcoming Trauma," serves as a powerful testament to the indomitable resilience of the human spirit and the transformative power of facing one's trauma head-on.

Hankins' memoir is a profound and introspective account of her personal journey through the darkest corridors of trauma. With unflinching honesty, she lays bare the depths of her pain, providing a raw glimpse into the immense struggle that trauma inflicts upon the human psyche. However, it is her unwavering courage and determination to confront her past that truly captivates readers.

"Overcoming Trauma" highlights the immense bravery required to face one's trauma, as it is through this courageous act that true healing can begin. Hankins emphasizes the importance of self-reflection, urging individuals to delve into the depths of their pain and confront the demons that haunt them. It is through this process of fearless introspection that the seeds of healing are sown.

The journey towards healing and recovery is by no means an easy one. It demands immense courage to confront the wounds of the past, to relive the pain, and to acknowledge the vulnerabilities that trauma has left in its wake. Yet, it is precisely this courage that paves the way for transformation and growth.

Hankins' memoir serves as a beacon of hope, reminding us that the human spirit possesses an unwavering resilience that can triumph over even the most profound trauma. By sharing her own story, she not only finds solace and healing but also inspires others to embark on their own path towards recovery. Through her words, she creates a sense of unity, assuring readers that they are not alone in their struggles.

The courage to confront trauma not only aids in healing but also serves as a catalyst for personal growth. It is through the courageous act of facing our pain that we can begin to rebuild our lives, reclaim our identities, and find newfound strength within ourselves. The transformative power of this courage cannot be understated, as it allows individuals to move beyond their trauma and embrace a future filled with hope and possibility.

In a world where trauma often leaves individuals feeling shattered and broken, it is crucial to recognize and celebrate the courage it takes to face it head-on. We must amplify the stories of resilience and bravery, for they serve as a reminder that healing is possible, even in the face of unimaginable pain. "Overcoming Trauma" stands as a testament to the triumph of the human spirit, urging us all to harness our courage and support one another in our collective journey towards healing.

Ultimately, it is through the unwavering courage to confront trauma that the human spirit finds its greatest strength. By embracing this courage, we can unlock the transformative power within us, transcending our past and forging a future defined by resilience, growth, and the unwavering spirit of triumph.

5 Tips to Manage Money Smarter

There's more to managing your money than paying your bills and successfully avoiding overdraft charges (although those are definitely steps in the right direction). Effectively managing your money takes time and planning, but the payoff may be a stronger financial future.

Create a budget. Some people avoid making a monthly budget because they think they don't need one. However, having a clear idea of the money coming in and going out of your bank account each month can help you make better spending decisions. A budget doesn't have to be complicated; it can be as simple as a spreadsheet that lists your monthly income and expenses. Be sure to consider long-term debt, like student loans, and treat your savings account as a payee you owe each month.

Track your spending. In a similar vein, it's a good idea to see where your non-bill-related spending goes. For example, you may stop by the grocery store more frequently than you realize, and each of those trips is likely going to cost you more than if you limited it to just once or twice a week. Many banks and credit institutions offer charts and graphs that break down your spending so you can see exactly where your money is going and use that information to make adjustments.

Research big purchases. What constitutes "big" may vary depending on your circumstances and financial status, but regardless of the dollar amount, doing some due diligence before purchases is a good idea. The average millennial will do 4.6 hours of research before buying a big-ticket item like a mattress or car, according to a survey conducted by OnePoll on behalf of Mattress Firm.

Millennials are also likely to seek input from others, with one in five consulting four or more people for their opinions on a purchase.

"Doing research before making a big purchase can make all the difference," said Timothy Mayes, Mattress Firm's senior manager of eCommerce merchandising. "There are several resources available such as online reviews, blogs and even guides on the best time to buy that can help save you money on larger purchases. If you find yourself overwhelmed with too many options, recommendations from friends and family are the best resources to help you narrow down your choices."

Prepare for emergencies. If a single unexpected event would cripple you financially, it's a good idea to build an emergency fund that could help you weather through a storm. A job loss, accident or illness would substantially alter your income, expenses or both, so having at least a few months of salary stashed in savings could make a major difference in how long that unfortunate scenario affects your life.

Finance purchases responsibly. Building credit takes time and responsibility, but if you don't ever borrow money, you won't have a chance to earn the rates reserved for exceptional credit holders. Financing a moderately sized purchase, such as a mattress, is a good starting point. It may be out of reach for a cash payment, but the balance you carry could be paid in a reasonably short timeframe. To build good credit, always make payments on time and make monthly payments larger than the minimum payment – which is usually just the interest – so you're actually paying down the principal.

Following these tips and taking advantage of product sites that offer resources and information on a potential purchase may aid in your long-term financial health. Find more information at MattressFirm.com/blog.

Timing for Success: Mastering the Art of Achieving Goals

Written by Vikki Jones

Timing is a critical element when it comes to achieving success and reaching our goals. Just like a well-choreographed dance, being in sync with the right moment can make all the difference. It's not just about working hard or having a solid plan; it's about understanding when to take action, when to pivot, and when to seize opportunities. Recognizing the importance of timing and mastering its art can significantly enhance our chances of success.

One key aspect of timing for success is knowing when to start. Oftentimes, we may find ourselves waiting for the perfect moment, waiting for all the stars to align. However, it's important to remember that waiting for the ideal conditions can lead to missed opportunities. Instead, we should focus on taking that initial step and starting towards our goals. As the saying goes, "The best time to plant a tree was 20 years ago. The second best time is now." By taking action and starting, we set ourselves on the path to success.

However, timing is not just about starting; it's also about recognizing when to make adjustments. As we progress towards our goals, we may encounter obstacles or unforeseen circumstances. Being able to adapt and adjust our strategies is crucial. Sometimes, it's about being patient and allowing things to unfold naturally. Other times, it's about making bold and timely decisions to steer ourselves back on track. The ability to assess the situation, gauge the right moment, and make necessary adjustments can be a game-changer in achieving our goals. Timing also plays a significant role in seizing opportunities. Opportunities often present themselves unexpectedly, and it's up to us to recognize them and act swiftly. This requires being alert, staying informed, and having a clear vision of our goals. By staying attuned to our surroundings and having a proactive mindset, we position ourselves to capitalize on these opportunities when they arise. As the saying goes, "Luck is what happens when preparation meets opportunity." By being prepared and having a keen sense of timing, we can create our own luck and open doors to success.

Furthermore, timing is closely tied to perseverance. Sometimes, success doesn't come overnight, and it requires patience and persistence. It's important to understand that

timing is not always within our control. There may be setbacks and delays along the way. However, by maintaining our focus, staying committed, and continuously working towards our goals, we position ourselves to be ready for the right moment when it arrives. Timing and perseverance go hand in hand, and together, they can propel us towards our desired outcomes.

To master the art of timing for success, it's crucial to develop self-awareness and intuition. Paying attention to our instincts and inner voice can provide valuable insights into when to take action, when to adjust our strategies, and when to seize opportunities. Additionally, learning from past experiences and observing successful individuals in our fields can provide valuable lessons and guidance on how to navigate timing effectively.

Timing is a critical factor in achieving success and reaching our goals. It involves knowing when to start, when to adjust, when to seize opportunities, and when to persevere. By mastering the art of timing, we can enhance our chances of success and set ourselves on the path to realizing our dreams. So, let's embrace the power of timing and use it as a valuable tool in our journey towards success.

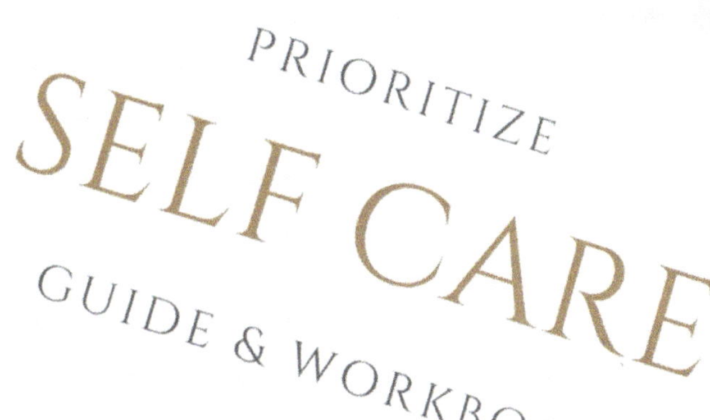

PRIORITIZE
SELF CARE
GUIDE & WORKBOOK

WRITTEN BY
VIKKI JONES
BARNES & NOBLE
BOOKSELLERS
amazon.com

What is
THE
SIMPLICITY OF
INDULGING
ONES PASSION

Ignite Passion for Your Work and Thrive

Passion Stimulates Value & Success If you have dreams, goals, and aspirational things you want to do with your life, go for it! Associate with people who will add to you and your goals versus take away from them. Get away from those folks that don't support your idea, and surround yourself with people that support and value you - help you grow.

@vmhmagazine

BOOSTING SMALL AND MEDIUM-SIZED BUSINESSES:

HOW AI AND CHATGPT CAN HELP

Written by Vikki Jones

Have you ever wondered how big companies always seem to have the upper hand when it comes to new technologies like Artificial Intelligence (AI)? It's because they have the money and staff to quickly jump on the AI bandwagon and make the most of it, while small and medium-sized businesses (SMEs) struggle to keep up. But shouldn't there be a way for smaller companies to increase their profits and tap into the full potential of AI too?

Well, the good news is that there is hope for SMEs to level the playing field and benefit from AI and the recently released ChatGPT. These fancy tech tools have a lot to offer, but it's understandable that smaller businesses might be hesitant to trust and adopt them. After all, they don't have an army of tech experts at their disposal like the big guys do.

But fear not, because there are practical ways for SMEs to embrace AI and ChatGPT without breaking the bank or feeling overwhelmed. The first step is education and awareness. SMEs need to take the time to learn about the benefits and possibilities that AI and ChatGPT can bring to their operations.

By understanding how these technologies can improve efficiency and productivity in specific areas, SMEs can start reaping the rewards.

Building trust is another crucial factor. AI might seem like a scary and unpredictable thing, but SMEs can ease their worries by partnering with reliable AI providers and starting with small-scale pilot projects. Seeing tangible results and success stories within their own industry will help SMEs gain confidence in AI as a valuable tool for their business.

Collaboration is key too. SMEs can team up with other small businesses or even larger companies to share resources, expertise, and navigate the AI landscape together. By working together, they can overcome the lack of technical talent and benefit from collective knowledge, which will ultimately level the playing field against their bigger competitors.

It's also important for governments and industry associations to lend a helping hand. They can offer incentives, grants, and specialized programs to support SMEs in implementing AI technologies. By creating an environment that promotes knowledge-sharing, collaboration, and innovation, policymakers can empower SMEs to fully embrace AI and unlock its potential.

Yes, the challenges of adopting AI and ChatGPT might seem challenging for SMEs, but it's important to remember that every new technology brings opportunities for growth and success. By seeking knowledge, building trust, embracing collaboration, and taking advantage of supportive policies, small and medium-sized businesses can harness the power of AI and ChatGPT to increase their profits, work more efficiently, and thrive in a competitive market.

PRACTICAL WAYS
SME'S CAN UTILIZE AI

Small and medium-sized enterprises (SMEs) can leverage the power of Artificial Intelligence (AI) in various ways to enhance their operations, improve efficiency, and drive growth.

1. **Customer Service and Support:** AI-powered chatbots and virtual assistants can handle customer inquiries, provide real-time support, and offer personalized recommendations. These AI-driven solutions can streamline customer interactions, reduce response times, and improve customer satisfaction, even outside regular business hours.

2. **Data Analysis and Insights:** AI algorithms can process large volumes of data quickly and accurately, enabling SMEs to gain valuable insights. By analyzing customer behavior, market trends, and operational data, SMEs can make informed decisions, identify patterns, and predict future trends. This helps in optimizing marketing strategies, inventory management, and overall business operations.

3. **Predictive Maintenance:** AI can help SMEs implement predictive maintenance strategies by analyzing data from sensors and machines. By detecting patterns and anomalies, AI algorithms can predict equipment failures or maintenance needs, allowing SMEs to proactively address issues before they escalate. This minimizes downtime, reduces maintenance costs, and extends the lifespan of machinery and assets.

4. **Process Automation:** AI-powered automation can streamline repetitive and time-consuming tasks, freeing up employees to focus on more strategic and value-added activities. SMEs can use AI to automate data entry, invoice processing, inventory management, and other routine tasks, improving operational efficiency and reducing errors.

5. **Sales and Marketing Optimization:** AI can enhance SMEs' sales and marketing efforts by analyzing customer data, identifying leads, and personalizing marketing campaigns. AI algorithms can segment customers based on their preferences, purchase history, and behavior, enabling SMEs to deliver targeted and relevant marketing messages. This helps in boosting conversion rates, increasing customer engagement, and optimizing sales funnels.

6. **Personalized Customer Experiences:** AI enables SMEs to deliver personalized experiences by analyzing customer preferences, behavior, and past interactions. AI algorithms can recommend products, content, and services tailored to each customer's specific needs and interests. This enhances customer satisfaction, loyalty, and drives repeat business.

7. **Market Research and Competitive Analysis:** SMEs can leverage AI to gather and analyze market data, customer reviews, social media sentiment, and competitor information. AI-powered tools can provide valuable insights into market trends, consumer preferences, and competitive intelligence. This helps SMEs make data-driven decisions, identify market gaps, and develop competitive strategies.

8. **Virtual Collaboration and Communication:** With the rise of remote work, AI-powered virtual collaboration tools can facilitate communication, project management, and knowledge sharing among remote teams. AI-driven solutions can automate scheduling, generate meeting summaries, and provide real-time language translation, enabling SMEs to collaborate effectively across borders and time zones.

Reinventing Yourself: Embracing Vitality in All Areas of Life for Maximum Benefits

The concept of reinventing oneself has become more important than ever. Embracing vitality in all aspects of life not only ensures personal growth and fulfillment but also positively impacts one's profession. By incorporating new things into our professional lives, we open doors to fresh opportunities, increased productivity, and overall success. This article explores the significance of reinventing oneself and how it benefits all aspects of life, including professional growth.

1. Unleashing Personal Growth:

Reinventing oneself is a transformative process that encourages personal growth in all areas of life. By embracing vitality, we challenge ourselves to step out of our comfort zones, explore new interests, and adopt a growth mindset. This not only enhances our skills and knowledge but also broadens our perspectives, making us more adaptable and resilient. As we reinvent ourselves, we become more confident, self-aware, and open to new experiences, ultimately leading to a more fulfilling life.

2. Achieving Balance and Wellness:

Vitality is not limited to professional success alone; it extends to all aspects of life, including physical, mental, and emotional well-being. Reinventing ourselves allows us to prioritize self-care, maintain a healthy work-life balance, and cultivate overall wellness. By incorporating new habits, such as exercise, meditation, or pursuing hobbies, we create a harmonious equilibrium that positively impacts our personal and professional lives. A balanced individual is more likely to excel in their career, build meaningful relationships, and experience greater satisfaction in life.

3. Boosting Professional Growth:

Reinventing oneself in professional settings is a powerful tool for career advancement and success. By incorporating new things into our profession, such as learning new skills, embracing emerging technologies, or pursuing additional education, we position ourselves at the forefront of our industry. This continuous growth not only enhances our expertise but also makes us more adaptable to

Embracing a Growth Mindset: Reinventing oneself is closely linked to adopting a growth mindset.

to changing market demands. Additionally, reinventing ourselves professionally opens doors to new opportunities, expands our network, and increases our chances of career progression.

4. Fostering Creativity and Innovation: Reinvention encourages creativity and innovation, both of which are vital in today's competitive world. By embracing new ideas, exploring different perspectives, and incorporating fresh approaches, we unlock our creative potential. This not only benefits our personal lives by sparking joy and fulfillment but also contributes to our professional success. A creative and innovative professional is more likely to find unique solutions to challenges, think outside the box, and stand out among their peers.

5. Stepping Out of Comfort Zones: Reinvention often requires stepping out of our comfort zones and embracing new experiences. Whether it's learning a new skill, pursuing a different career path, or exploring a new hobby, these unfamiliar territories push us to grow and adapt. By challenging ourselves and taking calculated risks, we develop resilience, confidence, and a broader perspective on life.

6. Discovering New Passions and Purpose: Through the process of reinvention, we have the opportunity to explore new interests, passions, and purposes.

By stepping out of our comfort zones and trying new things, we may stumble upon hidden talents or discover activities that bring us joy and fulfillment. This exploration helps us align our lives with our true passions and purpose, leading to a more meaningful and fulfilling existence.

7. Self-Reflection and Awareness: When we decide to reinvent ourselves, we embark on a journey of self-reflection and self-awareness. We question our beliefs, values, and behaviors, and assess if they align with our true desires and aspirations. This introspection helps us gain a deeper understanding of ourselves and identify areas where personal growth is needed.

Reinventing oneself leads to personal growth by fostering self-reflection, pushing us out of our comfort zones, embracing a growth mindset, expanding knowledge and skills, building resilience and adaptability, and discovering new passions and purpose. It is through this transformative process that we can unlock our full potential and lead a more fulfilling lives.